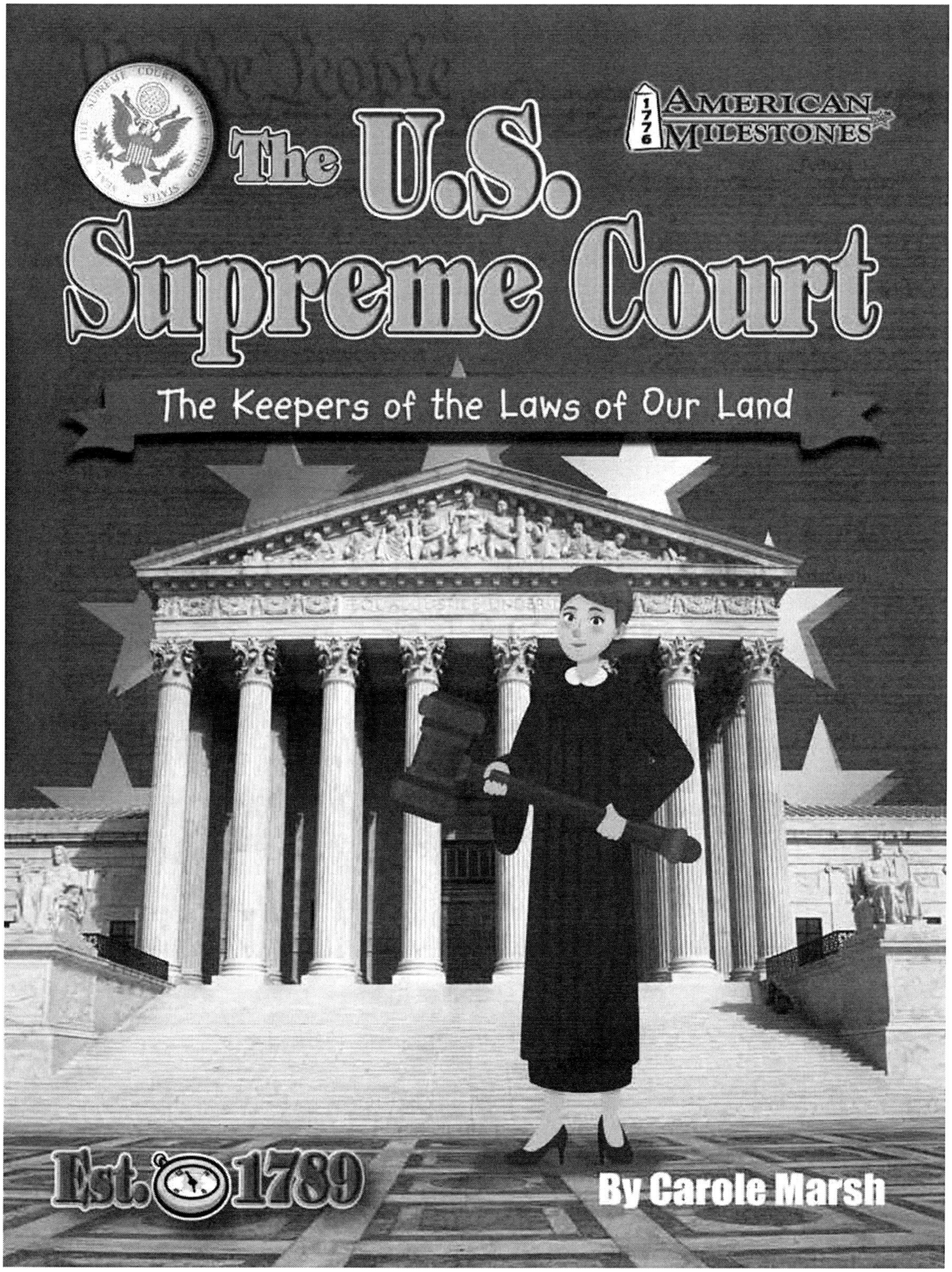
The U.S. Supreme Court
American Milestones
1776
The Keepers of the Laws of Our Land
Est. 1789
By Carole Marsh

I0892150

Published by

GALLOPADE™

800-536-2438
www.gallopade.com

Gallopade is proud to be a member of these educational organizations and associations:

American Booksellers Association
American Library Association
International Reading Association
National Association for Gifted Children
The National School Supply and Equipment Association
The National Council for the Social Studies
Museum Store Association
Public Lands Alliance
Association of Booksellers for Children
Association for the Study of African American Life and History
National Alliance of Black School Educators

More by Carole Marsh

American Milestones

The U.S. Supreme Court: The Keepers of the Laws of Our Land

The U.S. Civil Rights Movement: The Fight for Equality

Brown v. Board of Education: I Want To Go To School!

Declaration of Independence: Quit Bossing Us Around!

The Bill of Rights: It Can't Be Wrong!

U.S. Constitution: Sign on the Dotted Line!

Abraham Lincoln: America's 16th President

1000 Readers

Ruth Bader Ginsburg: Associate Justice of the Supreme Court

Sonia Sotomayor: First Hispanic Woman on the Supreme Court

Thurgood Marshall: Civil Rights Soldier

Lewis F. Powell, Jr.: Super Supreme Court Justice

Sandra Day O'Connor: First Woman Supreme Court Justice

Barack Obama: First African American President of the United States - 44th President

Donald J. Trump: 45th President of the United States

Joe Biden: 46th President of the United States

Biography FunBooks

Ruth Bader Ginsburg Biography FunBook

Sonia Sotomayor Biography FunBook

Barack Obama Biography FunBook

Big Cool USA

U.S. Constitution Coloring Book

Table of Contents

A Word From the Author

**Order in the court/the judge's gotta spit;
Who can't swim...better git!**

I remember this silly poem from my school days. My dad used to say it all the time. He was a Fulton County marshal in Atlanta, Georgia. Each day, he would go to court as the bailiff and start the proceedings by crying: "OYEZ, OYEZ, OYEZ, THE SUPERIOR COURT OF FULTON COUNTY IS NOW IN SESSION! JUDGE OBIEDOBIE PRESIDING! ALL RIIIIIIZZZZZZZEEEEE!"

Although as a kid I used to think some of this seemed silly and sounded funny, I knew that important things were happening in that courtroom. As I went through school, I learned that those things could affect people's lives—even including me, my family, and my future.

The law is important. Those who create, interpret, protect, and defend our laws are important. But the important thing is that they are OUR laws! That's why we should care about them, and about those who are the "keepers" of the laws of our land—The Supreme Court Justices of the United States of America!

These older, serious, perhaps stern-looking, men and women in their black robes may look intimidating, seem far removed from our daily lives, and maybe even be thought of (by kids!) as... **BOOOORRRRRING!** But nothing could be further from the truth.

We all know that America is so fortunate to be a democracy, a nation of laws and of law-abiding citizens. We know that our legal rights arise right out of the U.S. Constitution. We know that our nation's forefathers fought to get us such rights. Well, today, YOUR U.S. Supreme Court helps protect these laws for your use, keeps them refreshed for the changing times, and sorts out the major disagreements over what is right and what is wrong with laws.

These laws and these decisions affect all of our lives—yes, even the lives of children! Your rights as a student, person, and, later, as a parent, taxpayer, and more, are all affected by the decisions judges make.

They don't call them "legal opinions" for nothing! We each have an opinion. Which is right? The Supreme Court justices are people just like you and me. They have studied and worked hard to not only learn about the law, but also to have the wisdom to make the right decisions about the law. We count on them to keep it straight, sort it out, and make it work. It's a hard job and an amazing one!

Just imagine being one of a very few people whose job it is each day to be the "Keepers of the Laws of the Land"! Let's learn about OUR justices, OUR Supreme Court, and OUR role in this unique American institution!

Carole Marsh

OYEZ!

Our Newest Supreme Court Justice, Ketanji Brown Jackson!

Ketanji Brown Jackson

Ketanji Brown Jackson worked as a public defender and served on the U.S. Sentencing Commission before becoming a federal court judge. In April 2022, the U.S. Senate confirmed Jackson as an associate justice on the United States Supreme Court. Jackson succeeded Justice Stephen Breyer after he retired that June. Nominated by President Joe Biden, Ketanji Brown Jackson became the first African American woman to ever serve as a U.S. Supreme Court justice. She is also the first justice to have ever worked as a public defender. Public defenders represent people who are charged with a crime and cannot afford a lawyer.

Ketanji Brown Jackson was born in Washington, D.C. on September 14, 1970. She grew up in Miami, Florida. Her mother, Ellery Brown, became a school principal, while her father, Johnny Brown, became a lawyer. Jackson was in preschool when her father was studying to become a lawyer and would sit at the dinner table with him, coloring while he studied. "He had all his law books stacked up, and I had all my coloring books stacked up," she said. Jackson said that this experience is what gave her a love for the law.

In high school, Ketanji Brown Jackson was a star member of the debate and speech teams. She said competing in speech and debate prepared her for "future successes in law and life." She was also the senior class president!

Ketanji Brown Jackson attended Harvard-Radcliffe College, earning a degree in government, and Harvard Law School. While at Harvard, she met Patrick Graves Jackson, who was studying to be a surgeon. They married in 1996. They have two daughters, Leila and Talia.

After graduating law school, she clerked for two federal judges and for Justice Stephen Breyer—the same justice she would eventually succeed on the court. She also worked as an attorney in private practice, a federal public defender, and an attorney for the U.S. Sentencing Commission. The commission is a federal agency that develops federal sentencing guidelines to ensure that sentences are fair and equal around the country.

In 2010, President Barack Obama nominated Jackson to serve as a commissioner and vice chair of the U.S. Sentencing Commission. Two years later, Obama nominated her to serve as a federal district court judge in the Washington, D.C. Circuit. In 2021, President Joe Biden nominated her to serve as a judge on the U.S. Court of Appeals for the D.C. Circuit. She served there until she joined the U.S. Supreme Court.

The appointment of Ketanji Brown Jackson to the U.S. Supreme Court will have an impact for years to come. Americans will see how this justice will interpret American laws as time goes by.

More on Justice Jackson :

Before Jackson was born, her aunt was working with the Peace Corps in West Africa. Jackson's parents asked her to send them a list of African names for their baby girl. They picked the name Ketanji Onyika, which means "Lovely One."

In a college drama class, Jackson was the acting partner of future Hollywood star Matt Damon!

She said three important factors in her success are "hard work, big breaks, and tough skin."

"Do what you need to do before what you want to do" is a motto in her house.

During her confirmation hearings for the U.S. Sentencing Commission, she knitted to calm her nerves.

What do you think?

- If you wanted to become a justice on the U.S. Supreme Court one day, what steps would you have to take to realize your dream?
- What characteristics make a good judge?
- A Supreme Court justice must make very important decisions. How would you like to make decisions that affect the lives of so many people?

SCOTUS!
America's Highest Judicial Body

S = Supreme
C = Court
O = Of
T = The
U = United
S = States

SCOTUS is an "acronym" [you know, like CIA and FBI] for the highest judicial body in the United States. The Supreme Court of the United States is the tip top of our federal judicial system. You could say it's the leader of the pack when it comes to American law.

The Supreme Court is made up of:

- The Chief Justice of the United States
- Eight associate justices

The associate justices are nominated by the president of the United States. They must be "confirmed" by the U.S. Senate by a majority vote. This is said to be by the "advise and consent" of the Senate.

Once associate justices are "appointed," they serve a life term. Not like a life sentence in jail—they have life tenure, which means that they can serve until their death. This is conditional that they serve "during good behavior," and we know what that means. While many associate justices retire, many also serve their country until their deaths. Now that's dedication!

Associate justices may also leave their "lifetime" posts by resigning, or if they are convicted by impeachment for some reason.

These justices go to work at the Supreme Court Building in Washington, D.C. It is primarily an appellate court, but does have original jurisdiction over a few types of cases. In addition to being referred to as SCOTUS, it is also sometimes just called the High Court. Whatever you call it, it's a big deal and important. Taking responsibility for the laws of our land is a big responsibility and these hard-working justices deserve the respect of all Americans.

Justice William O. Douglas served the longest on the Supreme Court—36 years and six months.

Justice Sandra Day O'Connor was the first woman appointed Supreme Court Justice. She was nominated by President Ronald Reagan in 1981.

Congress decides how many justices sit on the Supreme Court. At first, there were only six. Since 1869, there have been nine.

Justice Thurgood Marshall was the first African American appointed to the Supreme Court. He was nominated by President Lyndon B. Johnson in 1967.

A Supreme Acrostic Puzzle!

S is for the Senate that must confirm them.
U is for upholding the U.S. Constitution.
P is for the president who appoints the justices.
R is for the robes the justices wear.
E is for the election that was contested.
M is for making tough decisions.
E is the effect the Supreme Court has on our nation.

Now see if you can write your own acrostic poems for the words court and justice. Use words that describe what the Supreme Court does.

C ______________________________
O ______________________________
U ______________________________
R ______________________________
T ______________________________

J ______________________________
U ______________________________
S ______________________________
T ______________________________
I ______________________________
C ______________________________
E ______________________________

A Short, Sweet, Supreme History

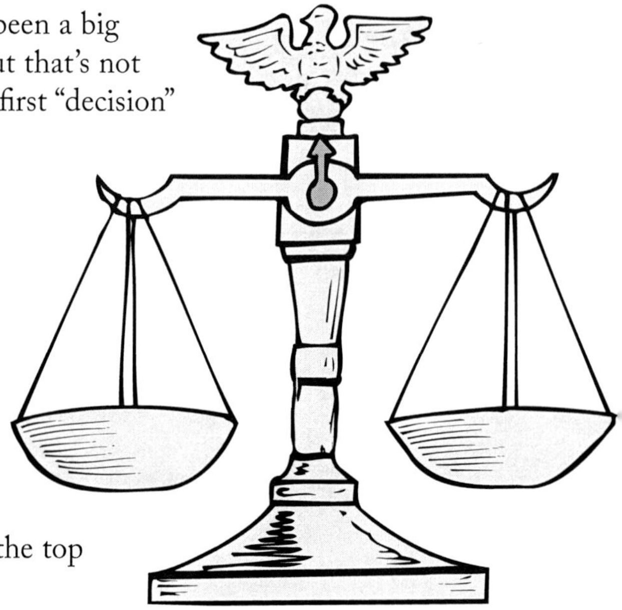

You might think that the Supreme Court has always been a big deal in a big building with big doings to do in legal land, but that's not so. At first, the early court only heard a few cases. Its very first "decision" on a case came in 1791.

In 1801, this court was declared the "supreme" arbiter of the U.S. Constitution. After the court made several important rulings, it was clear that the "balance of power" had shifted! The court ruled that it had the power to correct interpretations of the *federal* Constitution that had been made by *state* supreme courts. In other words, the "Supreme" Court really was now charged with maintaining the consistent and orderly development of our federal laws. The legal writing was on the wall—the Supreme Court was now a strong, independent, and "opinionated" body. It was the top dog in the law of our land!

After this, many cases helped define the scope and work of the Supreme Court. The important case of *Dred Scott v. Sandford* may even have had a role in the starting of America's Civil War. Many other cases began to help the Supreme Court see the changes necessary to make sure laws adhered to the Constitution. It was an important thing that state courts could have cases and "opinions," but that there could also be an "appeal" and that as needed, the Supreme Court could validate or override those decisions. And the Supreme Court decision would be FINAL!

Today, a lot of national news coverage is devoted to the workings of the Supreme Court. After all, the decisions it makes affect the lives of all Americans. Maybe YOU should pay attention to SCOTUS news!

You Make the Decision!

Fact or Opinion?

Put an F for fact or an O for opinion beside each statement.

____ 1. The Supreme Court is the highest court in America.

____ 2. Supreme Court justices have too much power.

____ 3. The Supreme Court helps protect the U.S. Constitution.

____ 4. A Supreme Court justice should be a native-born American.

____ 5. The Supreme Court should hear all appealed cases.

Meet Your Justices!

Below are pictures of each of our nine Supreme Court justices, and the date of their first day at their new job! Number the justices in order of when they began serving, with number one being the judge that has been there the longest. We've already done number one for you!

		Name	First Day on Job
______		**Brett Kavanaugh**	October 6, 2018
______		**Neil Gorsuch**	April 10, 2017
______		**Elena Kagan**	August 7, 2010
1		**Clarence Thomas**	October 23, 1991
______		**John G. Roberts**	September 29, 2005
______		**Amy Coney Barrett**	November 2, 2020
______		**Sonia Sotomayor**	August 8, 2009
______		**Samuel Alito**	January 31, 2006
______		**Ketanji Brown Jackson**	June 30, 2022

The Six Little Justices and How They Grew!

Six justices were too few. Ten justices were too many. Nine justices were just right! How did that come to be? In the beginning, Congress decided to place six justices on the Supreme Court. As the country grew, Congress thought the number of justices should grow too. Sometimes there were as many as ten! Finally, the Judiciary Act of 1869 set the number at nine, where it has remained to this day.

Year	# of Justices
1863	10
1790	6
1866	9
1807	7
1869	9
1837	9
1867	8

Order! Order! **The information above is all out of order. Using the chart, create a timeline showing the number of U.S. Supreme Court justices from the beginning until today.**

Jumping Through Hoops to Become a Justice!

Have you ever done or said anything embarrassing? Imagine FBI agents rummaging through everything you have ever written. Next, imagine them asking your friends and family all about you. If you were nominated to become a U.S. Supreme Court justice—that's what would happen to you. Then, snoopy senators (and all of America!) would hear all about it! That's what has to happen before someone becomes a Supreme Court judge.

The first step in choosing a new Supreme Court judge is the nomination. That's the president's job. The president can nominate anyone, but usually it's someone who shares the president's ideals and political views. But the president doesn't have the final say.

Then the Senate Judiciary Committee conducts hearings to ask the nominees questions about how they feel or think about different issues. When the hearings are over, the committee votes on sending the nomination to the full Senate. Most nominees are approved. Only 12 nominees have ever been rejected!

Perhaps you have seen television coverage of a Supreme Court confirmation hearing? The confirmation process often takes months, and hearings usually last four days. Members of the Senate ask nominees tough, and sometimes hostile or offensive, questions.

Think you might want to become a Supreme Court justice? Be careful what you say and do! It will all be revealed in your confirmation!

Getting to the Truth!
True/False?

Put a T for true or an F for False beside each statement.

____ A. Supreme Court justices can serve for the rest of their lives.

____ B. You must be elected to the Supreme Court.

____ C. The "junior" Supreme Court justice takes notes for everyone else in the court's private conferences.

____ D. The Supreme Court is part of the judicial branch of U.S. government.

____ E. The chief justice is the only justice who writes opinions.

Out to Recess!

The Senate has to confirm the president's choice of a Supreme Court justice. But if the Senate is in "recess," what's the president to do? The president can make a temporary appointment without the Senate's approval! This appointee can hold office less than two years before he or she has to be confirmed by the Senate to serve a full term. Recess appointments are controversial and no president has made one since 1958.

Good Behavior!

While good behavior may keep you out of the principal's office, it can do much more for a Supreme Court justice.

Justices are allowed to resign or retire when they wish. Congress may also remove justices through conviction and impeachment. This happened in 1805 to Justice Samuel Chase, although the Senate found him innocent and allowed him to stay on the Supreme Court.

But as long as justices maintain "good behavior," they are allowed to remain on the Supreme Court until they die. Talk about job security!

A Career in the Law?

Match the possible career you might have with the primary job done by this type of person. Then study hard!

1. attorney

2. prosecutor

3. judge

4. bailiff

5. public defender

a. a lawyer who represents people who cannot afford to pay for legal services

b. the person who prosecutes the defendant in a trial

c. the person who presides over a trial in a courthouse

d. a person who maintains order in the court

e. a lawyer who gives legal services for pay

The Supreme Court Gets a Home!

You might think that the United States Supreme Court had always had a very fancy and special home, but not so!

The Supreme Court first met on February 1, 1790, at the Merchant's Exchange Building in New York City. (Did you remember that at that time NYC was our nation's capital?!)

When Philadelphia became our next capital city in 1790, the Supreme Court tagged along, even meeting for a short time in famous Independence Hall! The poor court hardly had time to unpack as it then moved to Old City Hall, and after 1800 when Washington, D.C. became the capital, to various locations in the Capitol building.

In 1935, the High Court finally moved into its own majestic building! This building is a true Washington landmark that:

- Is four stories tall
- Was designed in a classical style
- Was designed by Cass Gilbert
- Is clad in marble, mainly from Vermont
- Includes the courtroom, justice chambers, law library, meeting spaces, a workshop, stores, cafeteria, and a gym!
- Has its own police force!
- Was remodeled in 2009 to add additional security systems

Many of our justices have spent a great part of their lives in this impressive building, working hard to make us a nation of law based on our Constitution. We all benefit from their hard work.

A Case of Cases!

Think one of your classmates swiped your favorite pencil? Want to take it directly to the Supreme Court? Not without a *certiorari!*

Your next question most likely is, "What's a certiorari?" Most cases come to the Supreme Court by way of petitions for writs of certiorari after they've already been heard in lower courts. Thankfully, these petitions are commonly called "certs." A certs petition is voted on at a session of the court called a conference. This is a private meeting where only the nine justices are present.

Certs are only granted for important reasons such as:

- to resolve a conflict in the interpretation of a federal law or a provision of the federal Constitution
- to correct a departure from the usual course of judicial proceedings
- to resolve an important question of federal law or review a decision of a lower court that conflicts with a previous decision

The court denies the majority of cert petitions and the decision of the lower court stands. The court receives more than 7,000 petitions each year, but usually hears only 100 or fewer.

When a cert petition is granted, each side has 30 minutes to present its argument and allow the justices to ask questions. The party that lost in the lower court is the *petitioner* and the party that won is the *respondent.* A majority vote of the justices decides the case. Finally, the court's "opinions" on the case are published in *U.S. Reports.*

Speaking of the Law!

Fill in the blanks using the words in the Word Bank below!

1. **An amicus curiae is a ___ ___ ___ ___ ___ ___ of the court.**
2. **Bona fide means in good ___ ___ ___ ___ ___.**
3. **Voir dire means to speak the ___ ___ ___ ___ ___.**
4. **Prima facie means at first ___ ___ ___ ___ ___.**
5. **Habeus corpus means to produce the ___ ___ ___ ___.**

Word Bank

FAITH
FRIEND
BODY
TRUTH
SIGHT

SCOTUS Basics

The U.S. Supreme Court is the highest court in the country. According to the Constitution, the function of the Supreme Court is to decide cases and controversies (disagreements). The Supreme Court interprets (explains the meaning of) our laws. For the most part, the Supreme Court hears appeals of decisions made in lower courts. The court reviews around 5,000 cases each year. The court decides about 150 cases of national importance and interest a year.

Our federal government has three branches—the judicial (the federal courts), the executive (the president and his Cabinet), and the legislative (Congress). The Constitution gave each branch a certain job to do. Each branch also has some power over the other branches. This is our system of checks and balances.

The members of the Supreme Court are appointed by the president and formally approved by the U.S. Senate. Supreme Court justices serve until they decide to retire, or until their death.

If a U.S. president has the opportunity to make an appointment to the U.S. Supreme Court, the choice is very important. The justices of the Supreme Court decide if our laws are constitutional (whether the law fits in with the U.S. Constitution). Their decisions can affect us for many years.

The Supreme Court opens a new term on the first Monday of October. The court hears arguments through April. The term ends when the Court releases its final opinion, usually at the end of June.

When a case goes to the Supreme Court, each side gets 30 minutes to present its case and answer questions from the justices. A large clock above the bench (where a judge sits in court) keeps time. The judges vote, then an opinion is written. Votes become final only when the opinion is issued.

Supreme Facts!

Established in	1789
Jurisdiction	United States
Location	Washington, D.C.
Composition method	Presidential nomination with Senate confirmation
Authorized by	U.S. Constitution
Judge term length	Life tenure
Number of positions	9, by statute
Website	www.supremecourtus.gov
Chief Justice of the United States	
Currently	John G. Roberts
Since	September 29, 2005

So It Is Written, So It Shall Be Done!

The Constitution of the United States of America is the supreme law of the land. State laws must conform to the state and United States constitutions.

constitutionality - being in agreement with the constitution of a government

Using the Word Bank, complete the sentences below.

Word Bank

LEGISLATIVE
JUDICIAL REVIEW
LAWS
SUPREME COURT
EXECUTIVE

The power of ____________ ____________ is an important check on the ________________ and ________________ branches of government. The constitutionality of _________ is determined by the __________________ ______________ of the United States and the state.

A portion of Chief Justice Marshall's statements from the *Marbury v. Madison* case of 1803:

"It is emphatically the province and duty of the Judicial Department to say what the law is. Those who apply the rule to particular cases must, of necessity, expound and interpret that rule. If two laws conflict with each other, the courts must decide on the operations of each."

According to this statement, which branch of government has the authority to interpret laws? Circle the correct answer.

EXECUTIVE LEGISLATIVE JUDICIAL

In the case of *Marbury v. Madison*, the Supreme Court granted itself the power to accept or reject the laws made by Congress. This was the beginning of judicial review. Some critics of the Supreme Court claim the court sometimes makes up new laws of its own, abusing its power.

What could be the danger of the Supreme Court having the power of judicial review? (Remember: there are only NINE justices on the Supreme Court!)

____

____

____

Supreme Court justices are allowed to serve for LIFE, or until they retire.

RETIRED

Who is the current Chief Justice of the Supreme Court? Which president appointed him/her?

Using the Word Bank, find the words in the word search.

Word Bank

JUDICIAL
LAWS
BRANCH
CHECK
COURT
GOVERN
ACTS

J	U	D	I	C	I	A	L
L	A	G	O	H	B	C	A
V	C	U	Z	E	R	T	W
B	R	A	N	C	H	S	S
T	C	H	I	K	B	U	X
Y	J	N	R	E	V	O	G

United States Court System

The United States has a separate court system whose organization and jurisdiction are derived from the Constitution of the United States of America and federal laws.

U.S. SUPREME COURT (Judges/no jury)
Jurisdiction: Appellate and Limited Original

U.S. COURTS OF APPEALS (Judges/no jury)
Jurisdiction: Appellate

U.S. DISTRICT COURTS (Judges and juries)
Jurisdiction: Original

Solve the math problem to find out how many justices are on the U.S. Supreme Court.

$(12 \times 2) + 6 - (30 / 2) - (2 \times 3) =$ ______ **justices**

The first meeting of the Supreme Court occurred in 1790, but there were no cases to hear so the justices went home and did not meet again for three years!

Complete the Courts!

Complete the diagram below describing the federal court system.

JUDICIAL BRANCH

FEDERAL COURTS

U.S. Supreme Court

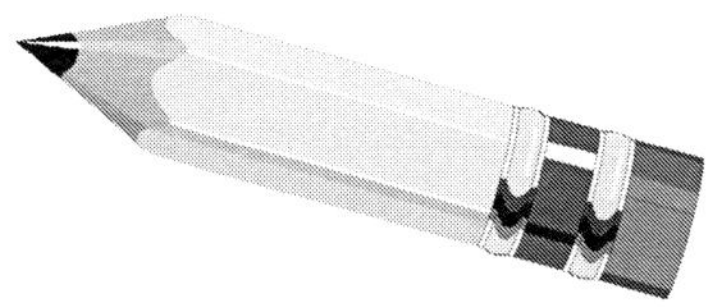

We've Got Our Eyes on You!

The Supreme Court of the United States determines the constitutionality of laws and of acts of the executive branch of government. This power is called JUDICIAL REVIEW, an important check on the legislative and executive branches of government. *Marbury v. Madison* established the principle of judicial review at the national level.

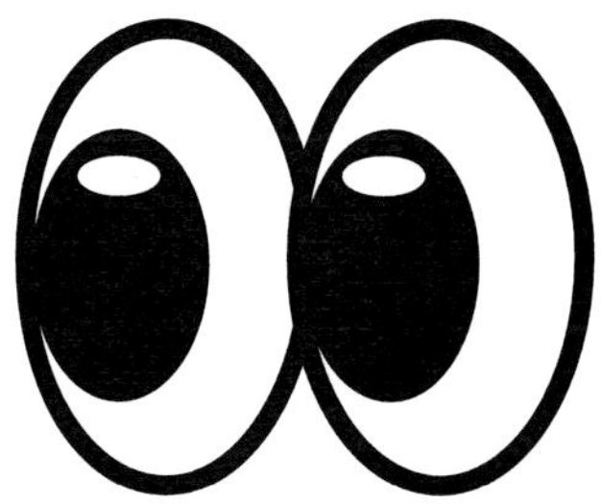

Starting with the Letter J

Starting with the letter J, cross out every other letter. The letters that are left will tell you the name of the president who appointed the most Supreme Court justices!

J G B E K O L R Q G S E T W V A C S D H G I H N P G U T W O X N

___ ___ ___ ___ ___ ___

___ ___ ___ ___ ___ ___ ___ ___ ___ ___

Do Make a Federal Case Out of It!

When you argue with a friend, who has the final word? When citizens disagree with each other or with laws, the Supreme Court has the final word. Here are some of the most famous arguments the highest court in the land has settled:

Dred Scott v.* Sandford: Ever wonder if a court case could start a war? This one certainly added fuel to the political fire that eventually became the Civil War. Dred Scott was an African American enslaved man who lived with his slaveholder in several states that did not permit slavery. Abolitionists, people who did not believe in slavery, helped Scott sue for his freedom in court. When the case went to the Supreme Court in 1857, seven out of nine justices voted that no slave or descendant of a slave could be a U.S. citizen. Since non-citizens could not sue in court, Scott had to remain enslaved. The Court also said the Congress could not stop slavery from spreading into the new territories. Abraham Lincoln spoke out against the decision. Slaveholders in the South liked the decision while anti-slavery leaders in the North did not. This brought the country one step closer to the Civil War!

Brown v. Board of Education: Look around you. Most likely, your classroom includes black students and white students as well as students from many other ethnic backgrounds. Thank the Supreme Court! Before 1954, black students and white students did not go to school together. The schools were supposed to be separate, but equal. That changed when the Supreme Court ruled that segregation in education, or keeping black and white children separated, was unconstitutional.

Other important cases that affect our lives include:

Miranda v. Arizona: It happens on all the cop shows! As the handcuffs are going on, the police officer reads the criminal his "rights" to remain silent and to get an attorney.

In re Gault: In this unanimous decision, the court ruled that juveniles (children and teenagers) charged with crimes have the same constitutional "due process" rights as adults.

Education for All Handicapped Children Act: Several Supreme Court cases led to this act which established the right to education for all handicapped children.

**v. (abbreviation for versus)*

Supreme Trivia!

Since 1800, Supreme Court justices have worn solid black robes. However, the earliest judges wore robes with a red facing similar to those worn by English judges.

The chief justice is the highest-ranking member of the court.

Does it pay to be a Supreme Court justice? You be the judge! Associate justices make about $265,000 and the chief justice makes about $277,000 a year.

Justices speak and vote in order of seniority. The most junior associate justice not only speaks and votes last, he or she answers the door and takes notes for everyone else during private court conferences.

When there is a tie vote on the Supreme Court, the tie-breaking vote is called a "swing vote." These votes are usually made by members who do not always vote conservative or liberal, but swing from one side to the other, depending on the issue.

When court is in session, the chief justice sits in the center with the most senior associate justice at his right and the most junior associate justice on the left farthest away from the chief justice.

While politicians are usually labeled by political party, justices are categorized as *conservatives*, *moderates*, or *liberals*.

Before the practice was stopped in 1891, justices who presided over the country's 13 Circuit Courts of Appeals were required to travel within the circuit or "ride circuit" to help local judges decide cases.

Since its earliest sessions, quill pens have been a part of the courtroom scene. White quills are placed on counsel tables each day the court sits.

The "conference handshake" has been a tradition since the late 19th century. When the justices assemble to go on the bench—each day and at the beginning of the private conferences—each justice shakes hands with each of the other eight.

Justices may serve until retirement, death, resignation, or impeachment.

In Your Opinion...

The 2009 appointment of Justice Sonia Sotomayor brought the first Hispanic American to the U.S. Supreme Court. The 2023 appointment of Ketanji Brown Jackson made her the sixth woman and first African American woman to become a member of the highest court of the land. As of 2023, four women sit on the U.S. Supreme Court.

Think about the diversity among the judges. Do you think it's important for the Supreme Court to fairly reflect the diversity among U.S. citizens? Do you think the Supreme Court does that now? Does this help the justices make decisions that are fair for everyone? How does it make you feel to know that *anyone* can be appointed to the Supreme Court, without regard to gender or race? Would you someday like to sit on the U.S. Supreme Court?

During Sotomayor's confirmation hearings, many questions were asked about whether her heritage might affect her decision making. The truth is her heritage should have nothing to do with it—justice is supposed to be blind!

Visiting the Court

Did you know you can visit the Supreme Court, even if you don't have a case?

- The Supreme Court is open to the public Monday through Friday from 9 a.m. to 4:30 p.m.
- Visitor programming is free and available on a first-come, first-served basis. Attractions include a courtroom lecture, visitors' film, and exhibitions. Visitors can also go to the cafeteria and gift shop.
- Yes, you can take photographs in the public spaces, but never in the actual courtroom.
- All oral arguments on a case are open to the public. However, seating is limited and available on a first-come, first-served basis. Visitors who want to attend an oral argument line up on the plaza in front of the Supreme Court building. Police officers handle seating visitors.
- If you attend an oral argument, keep in mind that you cannot wear sunglasses, identification tags (other than military ones), or inappropriate clothing.
- The Supreme Court is located at One First Street, NE, across First Street from the U.S. Capitol and across East Street from the Library of Congress. Street parking is extremely limited, but subway and bus lines are available. For more information, visit www.supremecourtus.gov.

A Legal Beagle Timeline

Sleuth this timeline and put it in order as these activities should rightfully occur.

A case moves through the Supreme Court in this order:

_____ A petition is voted on at a court conference

_____ A petition to review a case is sent to the court

_____ A selected petition is heard in briefings and oral arguments

_____ The court's opinion is published

_____ The case is submitted for decision

Glossary

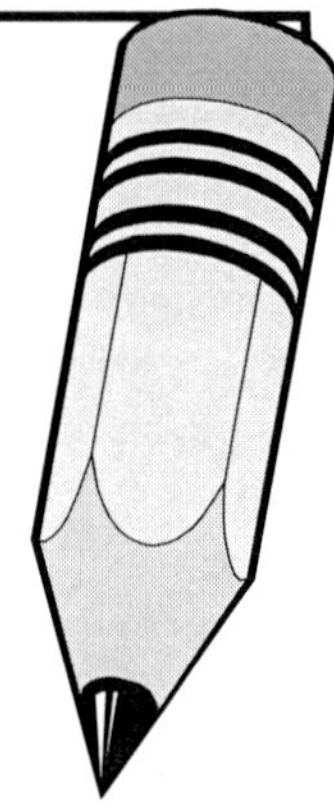

certiorari: Latin; a writ or legal document

petitioner: the party that lost in a ruling by a lower court

respondent: the party that won in a lower court ruling

conservative (politics): someone who believes in limited government, established political practices, and traditional social values; also called "right wing"

liberal (politics): someone who believes the government should be active in supporting social and political change; also called "left wing"

moderate (politics): someone who holds political beliefs that are not extremely liberal or extremely conservative

jurisdiction: the power to administer justice by hearing and determining controversies

amicus curiae: Latin; a "friend of the court"

confirmation: the Senate's process of approving a president's Supreme Court justice nominee

prima facie: Latin; "at first sight;" meaning that on the face of it, evidence appears to be true

ipso facto: Latin; "by the fact itself"

de jure: Latin; by law, according to the law

Pop Quiz

1. What is the title of the leader of the Supreme Court?
   - ❍ a. Highest Honor
   - ❍ b. Supreme Judge
   - ❍ c. Chief Justice
2. After Supreme Court justices are appointed, how long do they serve?
   - ❍ a. 4 years
   - ❍ b. 20 years
   - ❍ c. for life or until he or she resigns
3. Who nominates Supreme Court justices?
   - ❍ a. the president
   - ❍ b. the Circuit Court justices
   - ❍ c. Congress
4. What is the name of the famous Supreme Court case that many believe helped start the Civil War?
   - ❍ a. Roe v. Wade
   - ❍ b. Dred Scott v. Sandford
   - ❍ c. Brown v. Board of Education
5. In what city did the Supreme Court meet for the first time?
   - ❍ a. Philadelphia
   - ❍ b. Washington
   - ❍ c. New York
6. What is a tie-breaking vote cast by a Supreme Court justice called?
   - ❍ a. swing vote
   - ❍ b. moderate vote
   - ❍ c. stagger vote
7. Which justice takes notes and answers the door during private court conferences?
   - ❍ a. the valet justice
   - ❍ b. the most junior Associate Justice
   - ❍ c. the justice who arrived last
8. Which governing body has the task of confirming a Supreme Court nominee?
   - ❍ a. House of Representatives
   - ❍ b. the Senate
   - ❍ c. the FBI
9. How many Supreme Court justices are there?
   - ❍ a. 12
   - ❍ b. 9
   - ❍ c. 8
10. Who was the first woman appointed to the Supreme Court?
    - ❍ a. Sonia Sotomayor
    - ❍ b. Ruth Bader Ginsburg
    - ❍ c. Sandra Day O'Connor

Answer Key

Page 10: 1-F; 2-O; 3-F; 4-O; 5-O

Page 11: 1-Thomas; 2-Roberts; 3-Alito; 4-Sotomayor; 5-Kagan; 6-Gorsuch; 7-Kavanaugh; 8-Barrett; 9-Jackson

Page 13: A-T; B-F; C-T; D-T; E-F

Page 14: 1-E; 2-B; 3-C; 4-D; 5-A

Page 16: 1-friend; 2-faith; 3-truth; 4-sight; 5-body

Page 18: judicial review; legislative, executive; laws; Supreme Court

Page 19: Chief Justice John Roberts; appointed by President George W. Bush

J	U	D	I	C	I	A	L
L	A	G	O	H	B	C	A
V	C	U	Z	E	R	T	W
B	R	A	N	C	H	S	S
T	C	H	I	K	B	U	X
Y	J	N	R	E	V	O	G

Page 20: 9

Page 21: U.S. Courts of Appeals; U.S. District Courts: George Washington

Page 25: 1–A petition is sent to the Court; 2–A petition is voted on; 3–A petition has oral arguments; 4–The case goes to a decision; 5–The Court's opinion is published

Page 27: 1–C; 2–C; 3–A; 4–B; 5–C; 6–A; 7–B; 8–B; 9–B; 10–C